PUTTING THE OK IN YOUR 401K

How To Get Rich With ANY Retirement Plan

PUTTING THE OK IN YOUR 401K - How To Get Rich With ANY Retirement Plan

Carminucci Wealth Management
4 West Cross St
PO Box 998
Croton Falls, NY 10519-0998

Book design by:
Arbor Services, Inc.
www.arborservices.co/

Printed in the United States of America

PUTTING THE OK IN YOUR 401K - How To Get Rich With ANY Retirement Plan
Michael Carminucci

1. Title 2. Author 3. Finance

Library of Congress Control Number: 2019911500

ISBN 13: 978-0-578-55426-6

Praise For
Putting The OK In Your 401K

Sage advice in a concise understandable format. Enjoyed reading this practical and straight forward guide on how everybody can enjoy their "golden years" in comfort and confidence. I strongly recommend everyone to read this book and take the advice to heart to achieve peace of mind for you and your loved ones. Going to buy several copies and give them out as college graduation gifts—start early and retire in style!

— Tracy Christen Reimann, attorney-at-law

Practical and straight forward guide. This helped me to understand retirement plans and make changes to reduce my risk and maximize my returns.

— Dr. Lorraine Parker, Chiropractor

This is my go-to reference for investment information. Mike lays out in frank and easy to digest terms the benefits and pitfalls of a multitude of investment vehicles. It can be difficult to shake out unbiased advice from the noise of the investment world. This concise resource has been a godsend.

— Chris Harding, Business Owner,
IT Services & Computer Repair

PUTTING THE OK IN YOUR 401K

How To Get Rich With ANY Retirement Plan

MICHAEL CARMINUCCI

Carminucci Wealth Management

Contents

Introduction 1

Part 1: What Is a 401(k)?

Chapter 1: What Is a 401(k)? 5

Chapter 2: History of the 401(k) 12

Chapter 3: 403(b), 457(b), and Roth IRA 17

Chapter 4: 401(k) Catch Up 22

Chapter 5: 401(k) Withdrawals 24

Chapter 6: Preparing a Detailed Retirement Plan 27

Part 2: Investment Strategies and Common Mistakes

Chapter 7: Investing Basics 33

Chapter 8: Diversification and Consistency 38

Chapter 9: Different Funds 42

Chapter 10: Too Little Investment 48

Chapter 11: Market Volatility and Behavioral Finance 51

Chapter 12: Disciplined Account Rebalance 55

Chapter 13: Putting Short-Term Needs Second to
Long-Term Savings 61

Chapter 14: Leaving an Employer 63

Part 3: Using a 401(k) and Post Retirement

Chapter 15: Planning after Retirement 69

Chapter 16: Withdrawing from Your 401(k)................................73

Chapter 17: Social Security 77

Introduction

Traveling to exotic locales undisturbed by chattering crowds and suffocating modern connectivity; spending hours with grandchildren or a significant other while enjoying an occasional cocktail on the beach; constant golfing on a variety of the best courses—everyone has a unique vision of ideal retirement. One thing these visions have in common is that they require money. Sometimes a lot of money. Often more than you might imagine. A nifty little nest egg isn't going to cut it if you're looking to while away your later years dining out five nights a week while still having the money to pamper grandchildren. Saving enough money for a satisfying retirement is hard, and it requires long-term discipline.

People who put in decades of hard work deserve to spend their final years at ease, but financial turbulence, employer indifference, and simple ignorance often act against this right. Too many retirees end up with relatively little comfort because they did not, or could not, adequately prepare their finances while still at work.

Luckily for every future retiree, careful planning and understanding of the financial apparatus surrounding the process of saving for the future can yield remarkable results. Staying comfortable after your working years is an attainable goal for everyone who puts the time in to contribute what is needed.

This book is here to provide a thorough grounding in the steps a person has to take to retire at ease. Planning is essential; setting goals, calculating risk, and approximating your career—all are part of preparing yourself for retirement. Reassessment of your holdings is equally crucial as the aspects you originally planned for start to shift. People change jobs about every two and a half years, and that adds greater uncertainty to the savings process. You must be diligent with your retirement accounts and treat them with the necessary focus.

A thicket of federal bureaucracy and tax law is there to trip up anyone uneducated in the ins and outs of saving for their later years, and approaching those obstacles without the know-how to keep yourself and your money safe is inviting trouble. The cherry on top is fees, which apply to many financial transactions. Small percentages withdrawn and insignificant debits add up every time you move money around. If you are not careful, they can eat into your funds over time.

Navigating these factors requires preparation and knowledge guided by an expert hand. Here to provide that knowledge is Putting the OK in 401(k).

Part 1:
What Is a 401(k)?

Chapter 1:
What Is a 401(k)?

Planning for retirement is not limited to understanding 401(k) accounts, but they are the most common retirement accounts and thus are a good starting point. While most people with a steady job have a 401(k) in some form, they don't have a clear idea what it is. For starters, when people talk about having or managing a 401(k), they are talking about a type of retirement savings plan. 401(k) is the specific section of the tax code that outlines the taxation schedule for this retirement account, and, more importantly, allows for many of the numerous benefits of paying into that account. While there are several variations on a 401(k) plan—for instance some plans have an employer match the employee's deposits, something that we will cover in due course—the primary benefit is the postponement of taxation on contributions to the account. The government will not take a nickel of the money that ends up in a 401(k) until it is withdrawn as income years later. This deferment allows employees to reap the benefits of the investment portfolio, which will grow sometimes for as long as decades. People often choose 401(k) retirement plans with this benefit in mind.

Moreover, the employee is the owner of their 401(k). While some 401(k) plans involve employer contributions to the plan, the employer never has a claim to the money once deposited. Independence from employers and government influence is one of the aspects of 401(k) s that makes them so attractive, and jobs that come with 401(k) plans attached should be viewed in an accordingly positive light. Unfortunately, that benefit can be diminished by people making pedestrian mistakes with their plans. Knowing the intricacies of retirement plans is crucial, and here we can start to outline the basic stumbling blocks you will encounter on your journey to a safe retirement.

A simple problem to watch for is fees. The more transactions you make with your 401(k), the more charges you will accumulate from financial institutions. While these are more than offset by the benefits offered by 401(k)s, you should be aware they exist going forward, and consider their costs when moving money around. Other factors to consider are more complex.

Best Age to Begin

The first, simplest, and probably most important step in successfully saving for retirement is starting early. Chief among the problems people encounter with their retirement planning is waiting too long to begin. While, of course, a person can successfully prepare for retirement in the later stages of their career when they are generally making the most money, starting to save as early as your late twenties is a smart idea in order to capitalize on long-term compounded interest growth.

Albert Einstein has long gotten credit for saying, "Compound interest is the most powerful force in the universe." Historians occasionally dispute him as the source of this quote, but virtually no one disagrees with the sentiment. Long-term compound interest can generate incredible returns if the original investment is left alone. When you save using a 401(k) or another form of retirement account, an account manager will invest your money in a portfolio, usually consisting of a range of stocks and bonds. Over a long period of time, the fluctuations of the market will average out to a stable rate of interest, and your investment will grow steadily.

For those unfamiliar with finance jargon, interest is the percentage of your savings you gain by keeping them in a savings account. A retirement account with a 7% yearly growth rate would return $70 after holding a $1,000 deposit for a year. However, after that first year, if the money stayed in the account, the value would compound. That is, the $70 would remain and, after another year, the return would be 7% of $1070, or about $75. After another year, you would get 7% growth on $1,145, or about $81. As the years go by, the gains from compound interest increase to mammoth proportions. After ten years, that $1,000 would nearly double without you having to lift a finger.

If the math behind compound interest is a little too complex, the practical fact will do: consistently putting away money in a retirement account will, over time, yield massive returns. When you are in your early thirties, potentially beginning to manage a household for the first time, saving for retirement might appear to be an unaffordable luxury. For some people, this could be true. However, consider that, at a standard rate of roughly 7% or 8%, savings compounded every year for thirty years will increase by over 1,000%. Forty-five thousand would become close to half a million dollars. And that's without contributing anything in the meantime.

So, start saving as soon as you can. Whether that's when you are twenty-seven, thirty-seven, or even forty-seven, use compound interest to your advantage. It will pay amazing dividends so you are financially ready for a time when you need them most.

Managing Finances Early

Managing a retirement account when you are young is difficult, largely because you are unlikely to be making as much money as someone in a long-term position. Some people will still be chasing their student debt and thus will be reluctant to set aside even more income for another purpose. Others may not have jobs that offer robust IRA options. However, the aforementioned power of long-term compound interest should not be ignored.

Of course, the amount of money you save depends directly on how much you make. A good rule of thumb, therefore, is to try and have a year's salary saved and earning interest by age thirty. With that number in mind, you won't be too lenient and not deposit enough or go overboard and live frugally because most of every paycheck is tied up in a retirement account. Hitting the right numbers is easiest if you develop a rhythm for saving. Don't worry about dropping huge amounts into an account every two months; set up an automatic transfer—your employer can automatically withhold pay once you have access to a formal retirement account.

Risk Tolerance

When you are younger, you should not have a high tolerance for risk. If your pay is slim, don't risk wiping out the entire retirement account with risky investments. There is nothing more discouraging than getting used to saving for a year or two and then having a market downturn kill all momentum. Once you have a well-paying job and money piled up, adding a little risk to some of your holdings is a smart move.

Risk tolerance is key in managing a profile long term. Many people have a risk tolerance that is entirely too low. They see a downturn in markets and immediately want to flee to new funds that seem safer. And, as soon as those funds hit rocky seas, they send their money elsewhere. In the long run, keeping your money consistent with your buying and selling plans will yield the greatest result. Even if it might not feel like it, tolerating some risk will yield the greatest returns.

Of course, other people are far too tolerant of risk. They are the ones who see Google or Facebook in every new tech venture and are ready to sink all their money into it. These people need a little self-control before they drop all their money on an unproven dud. When saving for retirement, hitting your savings goals should not hinge on finding the "next big thing." Get-rich-quick decisions often yield "get poor fast" results.

The current craze of cryptocurrencies—unregulated decentralized online exchanges made popular by Bitcoin—are a perfect example of a situation where a future retiree must exercise reasonable risk tolerance. Prices for new cryptocurrencies can skyrocket with incredible rapidity. Those value explosions have created a slim class of overnight millionaires who emptied their savings at the right time. However, the same funds can crater just as quickly and with far greater likelihood and consequence. Recent studies have shown cryptocurrencies to be an unfortunate temptation for many. People around the world have lost massive portions of their retirement accounts by dumping their money into crypto.

Keeping Emotions in Check

You will find a running theme throughout this book, which is that success in long-term savings is all about keeping emotions in check. Often, the best practices may not be your first instinct. Doing the right thing, buying when you want to sell, staying steady on an issue that might not seem viable, and favoring steady, safe returns over a leap of faith are preferred behaviors whose degree of difficulty is based on personality. However, they are all based on maintaining control in the face of emotions stemming from financial opportunity and insecurity.

Maintaining these basic tenets is a challenge at first, but you will be rewarded for self-control later, when you need it most. While it might be difficult to forego some luxuries so you can afford to save, it may save you an extra year or two of retirement in the long run. Those are years you will be incredibly glad to have ultimately, especially as you reach an advanced age.

Chapter 2:

History of the 401(k)

A thorough grounding of the history of 401(k)s and retirement planning in the US would be a book unto itself. But we should stop here momentarily to traverse the timeline of the plan and to see how it has evolved over the years. Understanding the nature of how something started and why it changed will make you more attuned to the risks and rewards you will face.

The long history of American retirement planning harkens all the way back to the Revolutionary War. Soldiers who survived the war received lifetime combat pensions for their service—in part, yet another nod to Ancient Rome, the founders' favorite model for many areas of our government. Similar combat benefits were afforded to those who fought in the Civil War.

Noncombatants had few options regarding retirement plans until, in 1875, American Express created the first private pension plan for long-term employees who were "injured or worn out" by their work. This idea was incredibly popular and sparked similar plans to crop up with numerous other big businesses, such as Standard Oil and General Electric. Pensions encouraged lifelong loyalty to a company and generated a notable uptick in worker retention. In 1926, Congress acknowledged the popularity and facility of pensions by passing legislation granting corporations tax breaks on income passed on to employee pensions.

In 1935, President Franklin Roosevelt ushered in a massive shift in retirement planning with the passage of his New Deal. His reforms included the introduction of Social Security, the first universal public retirement savings plan in US law. With Social Security, people trusted that their government would help take care of them after they stopped working. This was a tectonic change in the government stance toward citizens in advanced age, and previous to Social Security, the idea of a 401(k)-style tax shelter for retirement planning would not have seemed possible.

In 1974, groundbreaking legislation came to the American worker's aid with the passage of the Employee Retirement Income Security Act (ERISA). This act's purpose was to regulate the growing number of voluntarily established private retirement accounts. ERISA contained numerous provisions to maintain the financial safety of retirees, including guidelines for retirement plan transparency, the formation of an appeals process for those who lost their investments, and enforcement of fiduciary responsibilities for account managers. Passing ERISA forever altered the government's stance on financial reforms for maintaining a safety net for retirees. The government has been amending, tweaking, and curtailing different benefits for decades since, and in doing so, paving the way for a 401(k) revolution to reshape retirement saving.

401(k)

The 401(k) is a relatively recent development in American tax law. It did not come into the picture until Congress's Revenue Act of 1978, which, among other things, amended national tax law to allow a 401(k) savings plan. Surprisingly, the original intention behind this taxation structure was not to provide employees with an effective method of saving their money. Legislators believed that the 401(k) alteration to the tax code would force highly paid business executives to limit their cash deferrals. For several years following the passage of the Revenue Act of 1978, the 401(k) remained an obscure detail of the US tax code; those aware of it often actively avoided it as an untested and therefore unreliable tax structure.

Then, in 1980, a retirement benefit consultant named Ted Benna considered using a 401(k) as a company-wide savings plan for workers at every level. The spark he conceived of that made this possible was the "employer match" system in which every dollar deferred from a worker's paycheck into the 401(k) retirement savings account would be matched by the employer. After failing to convince his clients of the brilliance of this idea, he decided to implement 401(k)s for the employees at his Johnson Companies, and the idea took off from there. The years following this saw an explosion in popularity. In 1996, the total funds in American 401(k)s hit $1 trillion; and as of 2018, they are closing on $4 trillion.

Government Response

Given the success of 401(k)s and the fact that the tax law that made them possible was not written for the purpose for which it was being used, not surprisingly, there was significant government pushback against the use of these retirement plans. While some of the developments were healthy—keeping an eye on new and untested financial instruments is not a bad idea and could have saved Americans a lot of heartache in 2008—many government efforts were an attempt to retrieve tax income they lost due to the nature of these savings plans.

In 1981, the IRS rapidly codified the rules covering how an employer could provide a 401(k) plan for employees, clarifing that regular earned income was allowable for use in 401(k) plans and not just profit-sharing income, as Ted Benna had originally suggested. This tweak was necessary for 401(k) plans' longevity and popularity, as profit-sharing income is only a small part of how most Americans earn a living.

However, it did not take long for Uncle Sam to get some of his money back. The Tax Equity and Fiscal Responsibility Act of 1982 saw a reduction in maximum allowable contributions to a 401(k) to $30,000 from $45,475. This was quickly followed by the Tax Reform Act of 1986, which induced further limitations on an individual's contributions to any form of deferred-contribution plan.

Eventually, steady inflation made the fixed limits on 401(k) contributions set in 1982 and 1986 untenable. Congress passed the Economic Growth and Tax Relief Reconciliation Act of 2001, which, among other things, significantly increased contribution limits. This increase in scope allowed 401(k)s to become a more powerful financial tool, as people could take greater advantage of tax deferment. The EGTRRA was crucial in maintaining the importance of these plans in the world of retirement savings.

These were the tentpoles in government action regarding retirement plans. They set the stage and act breaks for the story of American retirement to play out. Other innovations, such as the Roth IRA, 403(b), and 457(b) plans evolved out of the 401(k) and require their own chapter.

Chapter 3:

403(b), 457(b), and Roth IRA

The success of the 401(k) spawned numerous offshoots to suit certain situations more appropriately. While it was and is a versatile financial instrument, some people can benefit from different approaches to their retirement savings. Finding the right structure for your savings process can be key to a healthy retirement account.

403(b)

403(b) plans are largely similar to 401(k)s but focused on nonprofit, religious, or government organizations. 403(b)s actually predate 401(k) s by twenty-two years. In 1958, congress passed finance legislation that made 403(b)s available to 501(c)(3) companies—generally charities and nonprofit organizations. Before the introduction of 403(b)s, some employees of nonprofits were abusing their tax-exempt status to shelter their wages from government. The 403(b) came about to reign in that practice for nonprofit employees. Over the years, the 403(b) expanded in scope to cover a wide range of nontraditional, public sector, or tax-exempt workers, religious workers and public-school faculty being among those groups.

Because 403(b)s are exempt from certain administrative costs, they are more profitable than 401(k)s. They also have significantly higher deferral limits—how much money you can save tax free every year—than a traditional 401(k). For these reasons, 403(b)s are typically more profitable, although because of their limited eligibility, employers are less likely to use them.

457(b)

457(b) plans are another variant, more similar to a 403(b) than a 401(k), as they are available only to public sector employers and some nonprofit organizations with a 501(c)(3) designation. The chief distinction is, unlike a 401(k) or 403(b), 457(b)s do not offer a penalty for early withdrawal. Often, people who retire early need money out of their retirement account before traditional retirement age. Many retirement accounts impose penalties as high as 10% for withdrawing money before age fifty-nine and a half to prevent employees from abusing the account's tax-exempt status. However, this provision can be difficult on early retirees. Not so with a 457(b).

Some 457(b) accounts also feature a higher "double-limit catch up." As the name indicates, 457(b)s have a similar late-stage catch up mechanism as 401(k) accounts, but the limit on catch-up contributions is as much as two times higher. 457(b) accounts are the least used of all retirement accounts, largely because most employees, even in the public sector, do not qualify.

Roth IRA

Roth Individual Retirement Accounts are the most common alternative to 401(k), 403(b), or 457(b) retirement plans. Originating in 1997 with Senator William Roth, these accounts are contracts made directly with an investment firm, and they offer significant differences, some bad and some good.

For starters, contributions to a Roth account managed by an investment firm are not tax free. People typically set up a direct transfer from their bank account to an account with their broker who will help invest it. The government has already gotten its tax. The good news is that there are no taxes on money taken out of a Roth IRA, so all the growth from investment is untouched.

Roth accounts also do not offer any employer match. In a 401(k)—or one of its variants—employers will often match your account deferrals; that is, if you contribute $500 to your fund, the employer will contribute $500 of their own. This system works only in a 401(k), as your company's matches are tax deductible. Every time they contribute into an employee's retirement account, they can write it off come tax time. The same is not true for investment firms, so you won't catch them matching your Roth deposits anytime soon.

However, with a Roth IRA, your investment options are far more varied. When using a company-provided retirement account, you do not have much choice in how your money is invested. Understandably, most companies will stick to very safe investments, despite the low rate of return. Your money is more secure, but growth rates are likely to be on the slim side. (We will cover details of finance later on, but tactics are to focus on trusted mutual funds and to maintain a high bond/stock ratio.) Roth accounts operate at your discretion. If you prefer a riskier portfolio for the potential earnings, a Roth account can provide that option.

Roth vs. 401(k)

While the points above are important, choosing to focus your retirement savings on a Roth or a 401(k) account is largely about predicting what your tax situation will be like when you retire. If you expect to have a higher income when you retire, you should probably trust your money with a Roth IRA. Simply put, if you make more money, your taxes will go up, so paying taxes when you are making less money is the smart move. You should also consider whether you plan on working beyond retirement age. If that is the case, again, a Roth IRA is preferable.

One factor that may be difficult to predict long term but may be possible to glean with the help of a financial analyst is whether the federal government is trending toward lower tax rates. If you believe taxes will be set lower when you retire, a 401(k) might be the smart option.

This final point is more likely to come into play if you follow the increasingly common trend of maintaining a 401(k) and a Roth IRA simultaneously. Doing so is smart for several reasons. First, you have the aforementioned flexibility about which account you allocate money to each year. Based on your income, tax bracket, and level of employer match, the smart retirement account to choose may vary. Equally important, with two accounts, you have two sets of investments. A diverse portfolio will spread out risk and insulate you from economic downturns, something especially important as you near retirement. With a reliable return from your 401(k), you may be able to support a little more risk in your Roth IRA choices.

Ultimately, all types of retirement accounts share the same sets of potential problems and behaviors you can manage to get the best return possible. Whether dealing with a 457(b) or a Roth IRA or any other system we have covered—or will cover—be diligent with your savings, start early, and withdraw as little as possible before you actually retire.

Chapter 4:

401(k) Catch Up

We have previously discussed a crucial aspect of late-stage retirement savings: 401(k) catch-up. This tweak originated in 2001 with the Economic Growth and Tax Relief Reconciliation Act (EGTRRA). This act, introducing the concept of catching up, relaxes on contribution limits for workers over fifty. The idea behind catch-up is to help those who may not have saved as much as they needed at a younger age save more in a short period of time—something especially helpful for people who did not find well-paying jobs until later in life or who were dealing with significant financial burdens that limited their ability to save.

After turning fifty, you can significantly increase how much you are contributing to your retirement account. Some people with strong finances elect to set up a Roth IRA until turning fifty, and after that they shift Roth money into their 401(k). This is an option only for those making enough to fill multiple retirement accounts; some savers will not need to consider this possibility.

Of course, you do not need to utilize the catch-up process and can instead keep funds in your own investment portfolio or Roth retirement account. The way you handle your finances is based on your income, your attitude toward risk, and your personal knowledge of finance. If you feel comfortable navigating the stock market with or without a broker to guide you, then it could be a good option for you. However, never ignore the potency of the employer match aspect of your retirement plan. The catch-up process applies to any matches the company provides as well.

This decision should be made with the help of a financial counselor, if possible. They will evaluate your retirement plan options, income, tax bracket, and especially the condition of the market. If an economic downturn seems likely, you can save a lot of punishment by keeping your money out of volatile stocks and generally risky investment options.

Chapter 5:

401(k) Withdrawals

Retirement accounts are not meant to be withdrawn from early. They are designed to be most effective when left untouched until the correct time. Treating your savings like an ATM can completely undo the positive strides you've made from smart investments and employer match arrangements. Unless you are able to land a 457(b), your IRA and the government will likely penalize you for taking money out before a cutoff age; usually this is age fifty-nine and a half.

However, in some dire situations, withdrawing money from an account is the correct move. Retirement accounts can provide a backup fund in case catastrophe strikes and you need funds immediately. If possible, you should avoid this choice, but sometimes you have no other option. Luckily, the government and most savings plans recognize these situations as unusual and will allow you to make a withdrawal without taxes or other penalties.

Hardship

When you are facing dire financial straits, the retirement planning world dubs it a "hardship." In situations such as this, you may be allowed to take money from your 401(k) without an early withdrawal penalty. The IRS explicitly states that a hardship withdrawal is only allowed if the need is both "Due to an immediate and heavy financial need" and "Limited to the amount necessary to satisfy that financial need."

The first point is also known as the Safe Harbor rule, which discloses what "immediate and heavy financial needs" might be. These expenses include intensive medical care, housing, school tuition, disaster relief, or funerals; in other words, situations that are time sensitive and putting off a payment could result in calamity, such as being evicted or unable to repair damages from a hurricane.

Withdrawal limits, covered in the second stipulation, are simple. You cannot take out more money than what is necessary to cover Safe Harbor. An employee needs only to explain in a written-and-signed document what their need is and how they have exhausted their options for other avenues of funding—insurance, liquidation of personal assets, or loans—and an employer legally must relinquish the necessary amount of your savings. The withdrawal will still be taxed, but if you meet the required conditions, you can take money out of your 401(k).

At the risk of being redundant, this option is a last resort. Make sure to use all potential sources of income before emptying a retirement account. Many future retirees discount the negative impact a lack of savings can have, but unless working well past seventy is a goal, leave savings alone. Too many people use their 401(k) as a cash machine and borrow consistently from it, dramatically effecting their future.

Taking Out a Loan

Each type of plan has withdrawal options that are taxable but often contain provisions for hardship that will avoid the early withdrawal penalties. However, despite the lack of taxes on hardship-specific withdrawals, people need to be aware that they should never take early withdrawals out of these retirement accounts unless it's absolutely necessary.

In light of this information, taking out a loan against a 401(k) might seem like a good idea if you find yourself in a financial hardship. While it does avoid the immediate downsides of withdrawing from your 401(k)—namely the negative impact a lower principal amount will have on long-term earnings—hardship loans are accompanied by their own set of problems.

First, if you are in a hardship position, it will often be very difficult to obtain a loan. Many money lenders will be averse to the risk hardship conditions typically create. And if you can secure a loan, the interest rate will likely be extremely high, which can cause more problems than it fixes. This is, incidentally, something to always be aware of when you are borrowing money. Short-term fixes are often too good to be true and can create much worse long-term problems.

Second, while loans against a 401(k) are not initially taxable, if you do not pay back the entirety of the loan before cashing out a 401(k) or rolling it over into another fund, the loan becomes classified as a "distribution," and the government will tax it. Other earnings from mutual funds and capital gains are also classified as distributions and are subject to state and federal taxes.

Chapter 6:

Preparing a Detailed Retirement Plan

A major step that can make a comfortable retirement possible is preparing a clear plan for how you will save money now. Knowing how and when to allocate funds, as well as how much you want to defer each paycheck, will make the entire process easier. The first key step to a good retirement plan is to set goals. Depending on your financial security and how your plan is structured with your employer, 15% of your income is a good baseline for withholding. If this is greater than your plan's limit, then invest in a Roth IRA as well as your 401(k), 403(b), or 457(b).

Once you have the percentages mapped out, estimate the dollar value of hitting your savings goals. While estimating how much money you will be making in a few years can be difficult, especially at a young age, it is good practice; your income will stabilize as you get set in a career track.

After these steps, do a little math and see how much your savings will yield. A quick search online should turn up simple sites that can do this for you with a little information. For instance, if you are hoping to put $5,000 in an account with an average 7% return on investment (ROI), you will have $37,000 in five years. With an employer match, that's only $2,500, a $12,500 investment, which will almost triple. Once you know how each investment should turn out, you can adjust your saving goals accordingly.

A savings plan is as much about consistency as it is starting with clear goals. Financial profiles do not stay the same for long periods of time. Your income and costs almost certainly will fluctuate a great deal during your working life. Every time you face a major life change, or even slight disruptions in your payment schedule, keep an eye on your retirement accounts. The prudent move is to check and refocus your retirement plan every month. Whether you get a raise or encounter a new healthcare cost, your retirement goals will always be in flux. Do not forget, when planning for later years, expect higher bills at the doctor's office. Age can be rough on some bank accounts.

Most experts agree that goal setting is the most important part of creating a retirement plan. Once you have the goal in place, the next step is creating benchmarks. Consider setting certain age ranges on when you should be hitting a specific percentage of your goal. Retirement authorities have come to a strong consensus that a good saver on track to meet their overall goal will have at least 50–55% of the total savings by age fifty. While this is not always possible given the curveballs life can throw at us, that percentage should be your goal. The next ten years beyond age fifty should considerably grow your value, bringing the total worth of your retirement portfolio to close to 90% of your goal. Once you reach that point, you should move considerable portions of your money into stable index funds.

At that point, another few years of steady but measured growth should get you to your retirement goal around age sixty-five. That is a reasonable expectation, not overly ambitious or reserved. If you work these benchmarks comfortably into your retirement plan, you will base your saving on simple, achievable goals, and be well on your way to a comfortable retirement.

Part 2:
Investment Strategies and Common Mistakes

Chapter 7:

Investing Basics

Investing is, of course, a key part of retirement saving. The immense potential of long-term financial growth is only possible with diligent investment practices. However, choosing an investment portfolio is also an often highly complex and potentially confusing process. If you don't adequately prepare yourself for the situation, you could easily make costly errors.

Before going any further, it is crucial we recognize the risk inherent in your investing practices. The simple underlying fact of all investing is that making greater gains comes with greater risk. When you play it safe with stable value funds and other steady purchases, you do not have nearly the potential for growth as you would with stocks, which rise higher and fall lower. We will go over how to manage the unpredictability of stocks later on, but for now, understand that including some uncertainty in your portfolio is not optional; you would not meet the requisite long-term growth objectives without higher-risk/higher-return stocks. This is an unavoidable aspect of 401(k)s, IRAs, and other retirement accounts. You prepare yourself for the reality that stock prices rise and fall, and, while you can offset that volatility with the proper investing behavior, it is a reality you have to come to grips with.

What makes investing so difficult is the many variables to consider. Choosing stocks and bonds requires answering numerous questions to garner the necessary information. You must identify your objectives, set a timetable for your procurements, and recognize your preferences. All these options affect how you invest, and they can conflict with one another.

Investing also requires numerous transactions facilitated by financial institutions, and these steps often come with fees attached. Investing your money, setting a portfolio, and keeping your assets balanced (also known as rebalancing, which we will cover later on) necessitate actions that you will be charged for. Efficiency and diligence with your activity will pay off.

Identifying Objectives

Before you set out to invest your money, you need to consider what your savings goals are. Figuring out how much money you will need when you retire is key. It is the target you will have to hit, and the rate of interest on your portfolio determines how much you need to put away every year. If you set a high goal for your retirement fund, you will need to allocate your money in stocks with a higher rate of return. Again, this will come with a greater degree of volatility.

Setting a Timetable

The timetable in which you have to let your investments grow is also significant. If you are thirty-five and just beginning to save for retirement, look for stocks that will show rapid growth, as opposed to safe, established issues that will not generate enough return to hit your goals on time. This is also the time to carefully consider when you plan on leaving the workforce and cashing in your 401(k). Some people prefer to work and may stay active until their mid-seventies. Others will start toning their work life down much earlier and seek a life of leisure. Base your timetable off of this setting.

Recognizing Preferences

This point is somewhat secondary to the other determinants, but investing based on your personal preferences is reasonable. Some people are interested in supporting green energy companies; others might want to help boost artistic endeavors or focus their money in practical issues focused in the manufacturing sector. While it is unwise to make too much of a shift in one direction just because you, for instance, are interested in fly-fishing, some adjustments are reasonable when you are making final choices in the portfolio. Your dollars will have an impact on others as well as yourself, and taking time to consider that isn't a bad thing; even if it will ultimately take a backseat to practical concerns.

Risk Tolerance

A final key factor in investment behavior, something that impacts investors far too much, is risk tolerance—how much risk an investor is willing to tolerate in the market. Many people suffer from an inability to tolerate risk during times in which markets are in flux. They see the value of their acquisitions decrease, and they assume they should change up the entire portfolio. This is a false impression, often originating in blaring financial news segments or panicked magazine articles that manufacture apocalyptic narratives every time the economy takes a dip.

The fallacy behind a low-risk tolerance attitude usually comes from not knowing two basic financial facts. First, some market decline is healthy. If every stock was constantly soaring for years on end, that would signify underlying dangers in the financial instruments in play. Somewhere, bankers or brokers or regulators or risk evaluators aren't doing their jobs. A sound economy will regularly experience periods of reasonable decline. This is called contraction, and it needs to happen in order to, among other reasons, keep the value of currency under control. If you hold your investments steady and continue to add to your portfolio even during times of contraction, in the long run, your savings will grow to the extent you need.

Second, people look at a lowering of the value of their stock as a direct hit to their retirement account. Again, this is largely reinforced by mainstream financial media as a tactic to draw more viewership. In reality, the right way to look at lower stock prices is as an opportunity for your deposits to go further. If a stock is cheaper, the money you're investing every month will buy more. In the book Advances in Behavioral Finance, Richard Thaler writes, "Although the stock market was long thought to be a random walk, and thus unpredictable, numerous researchers have found that over long horizons [several years] the returns on the stock market are least somewhat predictable. Specifically, when stock prices are very high . . . then subsequent returns tend to be low." Low prices can, therefore, be your time to strike. When the market returns to full strength, you will have gained a great deal in retirement value. Probably the most well-known stock tip is "buy low, sell high." Think of your retirement savings in that vein, and some temporary drop in stock value is a chance to increase your buying power.

So, your risk tolerance is essentially your ability to "hang on" when the market is not doing as well as you would like, and a high level of risk tolerance is certainly a good thing. Once you have carefully created your stock portfolio, it is nearly always the correct decision not to withdraw early, despite what may be happening in the markets in the short term. Adjusting on a quarterly or biannual basis is enough of a response to market activity, and it should be done very carefully. After you have done all the work and consulted with experts to craft a portfolio that fits your needs, trust the process. Don't give in to media hype about impending market trends; over the course of decades, you will reap the benefits of not giving in to low risk tolerance.

These are the necessary considerations to make when preparing your investment portfolio. However, this knowledge isn't useful unless you understand what financial tools you have to use to accomplish your goals. You have from a litany of various fund types and investment structures to choose. The following chapters will address these.

Chapter 8:

Diversification and Consistency

Probably the most basic concept in investing is known as diversification. Diversifying your investment portfolio means including many different types of stocks and bonds. That way, if some lose value, others may continue to gain or at least maintain their value, minimizing potential loses. A well-diversified group of stocks will steadily rise in value along with the overall stock market. If you do not diversify your portfolio, then one or two stocks losing value might tank your retirement account value. A good mix of different issues will spread out risk and keep your portfolio insulated from localized market problems.

Diversification is one major reason that index funds are a good option for retirement accounts. We will cover index funds later on, but simply put, their main benefit is security due to a high level of diversification. Think of investing as a tightrope act. The goal is to maintain a balance of weight distribution on either side of the wire. Diversification is a wire walker's pole. If weight starts to shift to one side of the wire, the walker will move their pole to the other side so the weight on either side of the wire is evenly balanced and they will not fall. Diversification works in much the same way. If one stock dips too much to one side, others, unaffected by the factors driving down that stock, will swing in the other direction. A diversified portfolio has issues pulling in opposing directions and so remains centered, continuing to grow slowly, like a tightrope walker moving steadily forward on their wire.

Opposite of diversification is the principle of consistency, or how much you stick to investing in certain funds. While diversification is a good way to keep your assets safe and growing even in a down market, the concept can be taken too far. If you spread all of your investment capital across too wide a range of stocks or funds, you will hinder any chances at major growth. Some consistency is necessary to maintain your position.

Diversification also certainly has its limits. When you diversify a portfolio, you eliminate most of what is known as idiosyncratic risk. That is risk associated with a single stock. A simple example of idiosyncratic risk is a company that turns out to be fraudulent. That is risk specific to that stock, not an entire group of stocks or an index of the whole market.

However, diversification cannot combat risk across larger swaths of the market. Major events, such as natural disasters that destroy access to a crucial resource, will take down entire fields of a market. Large index funds, which we will cover soon, are diversified over the entire stock market, but even they are not immune to risk, as the 2008 financial housing crisis so clearly illustrated. When the entire market is hit, diversification loses its power. In situations like that, the best a person can do is whether the storm until the market recovers—as it ultimately has. As bad as things were for many years, the market corrected, and the retirement portfolios regained value.

Ultimately, diversification is critical, but you can go too far in applying it. With smart planning, you can choose a portfolio that is relatively safe. However, in reality, risk is part of investing. No stock is perfectly safe, and you will have to grow accustomed to that when you are saving for retirement. In other words, your risk tolerance will likely grow, and you will become more comfortable with flexible or even volatile stock issues.

Modern Portfolio Theory

While diversification is not a new concept by any means, its emphasis in modern financial instruments, especially in long-term savings portfolios, was something of a revelation relatively recently. In 1952, Harry Markowitz published "Portfolio Selection" in the Journal of Finance, outlining the principles of diversification that would come to be known as Modern Portfolio Theory, or MPT. He wrote, "We . . . consider the rule that the investor does (or should) consider expected return a desirable thing and variance of return an undesirable thing." Markowitz believed that the potential for unreliable returns was unavoidable in a single stock, but negligible in a group of relatively disconnected stocks. Maximizing your returns was directly related to minimizing variance, so diversification was much more important than trying to find a "hot new stock."

In a review of Markowitz's work, "The Legacy of Modern Portfolio Theory," Frank Fabozzi summarizes these ideas as we now use them. "Conventional wisdom has always dictated not putting all your eggs in one basket. In more technical terms, this adage is addressing the benefits of diversification. MPT quantified the concept of diversification, or 'undiversification,' by introducing the statistical notion of a covariance, or correlation. In essence, the adage means that putting all your money in investments that may all go broke at the same time, i.e., whose returns are highly correlated, is not a very prudent investment strategy—no matter how small the chance is that any one single investment will go broke."

As Markowitz's paper shone focus on diversification, finance experts created a variety of investment tools to capitalize on his principles. Some are obscure and beyond the scope of this text. However, many are incredibly useful, even to common investors. We will cover these, specifically types of funds, in the next chapter.

Chapter 9:

Different Funds

Once you have considered these factors, you will need to choose the funds that fit the goals you have set. Most 401(k)s have a number of investment options, each fund having a different objective and fee structure. The three most common funds are index funds, target allocation funds, and exchange-traded funds. Each has its own strengths and weaknesses, and understanding those properties will prepare you for a lucrative and secure retirement process. While the array of options can be confusing and even a little overwhelming, if you put in the time to understand the tools at your disposal, these financial instruments will enable you to make the most of your money.

Exchange-Traded Funds

Exchange-traded funds are made up of groups of stocks assembled around some common property, such as a specific market or type of risk. In many ways they are similar to regular stocks. They require no minimum investment, are fairly inexpensive, and are valued based on the demand of the comprising assets. ETFs offer the benefit of some diversification, as they are made up of numerous stocks. However, their focused nature still allows for the possibility that all underlying stocks will crater simultaneously. For instance, an ETF based on a tranche, or group, of fossil fuel stocks will lose tremendous amounts of value if there is an innovation in solar power. So-called "disruptive technologies" are often the cause for massive shifts in value in ETFs.

However, like the stocks that comprise it, an ETF can grow more rapidly than other types of funds. Just as changes in technology or new business models can hurt an exchange-traded fund, these evolutions can help. While many ETFs are fairly stable—one based on the value of the pharmaceutical industry, for instance—others have the potential for significant and steady growth. As artificial intelligence becomes an increasingly great influencer in modern society, ETFs focused on that technology become more valuable. Many experts expect AI funds will be healthy long-term investments.

Index Funds

Index funds are a type of exchange-traded fund. The two share many characteristics, such as a high level of diversification and low expenses relative to straightforward and often more volatile funds. However, an index fund is not nearly as focused as a generic ETF. Whereas ETFs emphasize specific areas, indexes are market-wide evaluations and so are incredibly stable. Indexes can respond strongly to government tax and finance policy, as they are generally composed of powerful corporations in a range of different fields. Other ETFs may contain smaller companies that potentially do not face the same benefits

Index funds are probably the most well-known funds, as the largest of them are often used as measures of the health of the stock market.

The two you may have heard of are the Dow Jones Industrial Average, often referred to as simply "the Dow," and Standard and Poor's 500, often "the S&P 500." The Dow is made up of 30 "blue-chip stocks" chosen by editors of the Wall Street Journal. If you are not familiar, blue-chip stocks are the largest and most stable stocks on the market, often with market valuations in the billions of dollars. For reliable, long-term growth, investing in the Dow Jones Industrial Average is smart, and many choose to allocate large parts of their retirement funds in the Dow.

The S&P 500 is a much larger index. Standard and Poor's is a ratings agency. They determine the health of a financial instrument in the market by giving it a rating from BBB to AAA, and investors use this information to inform the buying and selling decisions. The S&P 500 index is a group of the market's five hundred largest and most robust stocks chosen by a council at S&P. Because the S&P index contains more stocks, it is even more stable than the Dow.

Experts in finance often argue over which index is a better measure of market health. Standard and Poor's change the criteria they use to select stocks more often than the editors of The Wall Street Journal. However, some feel that the Journal is biased toward certain stocks and that their decisions are more than just financial. Regardless of the truth of these arguments, it is indisputable that, for the past five years, the S&P has been outperforming the Dow Jones in growth by a considerable margin.

Target Allocation Funds

Target allocation funds, or target date funds, are another type of exchange-traded fund. Like ETFs and index funds, TAFs are a diversified portfolio of stocks designed to maintain a high level of stability. Unlike other funds, target allocation funds have built-in time constraints and markers that gradually ratchet down any risk. TAFs are ideal retirement funds in many ways. The added factor of a time component makes TAFs more complex than other funds, but many of the operations are ones a retirement investor should be doing anyway. It is advisable to begin by allocating your savings in riskier funds with a higher return, and then to lower that risk in later years.

These funds are sometimes referred to as "life-cycle funds," as they adjust risk on an age-based strategy. This mechanism is their primary difference from other normal or "balanced" funds. Annamaria Lusardi writes in Overcoming the Savings Slump, "Unlike balanced funds, however, life-cycle funds do not keep their target mix constant over time; instead, they change their target mix according to a predefine 'roll-down' schedule until they reach a date called the target date or target maturity date of the fund. This roll-down schedule becomes more conservative over time in the sense that it tilts the target mix away from equities and toward bonds and cash."

Choosing a Fund

With all these varieties of funds, deciding which ones to emphasize can be daunting. One final distinction may help make this decision more clear cut. When investors compare differences between target allocation funds, index funds, and exchange-traded funds, they often focus on whether you want a fund that is passive or actively managed. This essentially refers to the level of change the fund goes through. Actively managed funds are usually run by a portfolio manager who changes them regularly in order to hit the investor's goals—while staying within their risk tolerance range. Target allocation funds are an actively managed fund.

Passive funds, on the other hand, do not change. The investor or portfolio manager carefully selects the stocks that go into the fund, and they are left alone to mature. Index funds are a passive fund. They rise and fall, but ideally, with a good portfolio, will—and usually do—grow significantly.

Choosing between active and passive funds is essentially a question of how well an active fund might be managed. While passive funds are quite popular now, in part due to Markowitz's Modern Portfolio Theory and in part due to a good track record, well-managed active funds can yield higher results. Smart portfolio managers can react to or even predict changes in the market and shift the stock composition in response. Passive funds to not allow for any kind of deft fiscal maneuvering that actively managed funds do.

One certainty is this: if you want an actively managed retirement fund, do not do it yourself. Good portfolio managers might be able to beat the Dow or the S&P, but you can't. This is not a knock on the general public's intelligence but a testament to the difficulty of reading the market. Consider the years of schooling and experience, and the near constant attention it takes for a portfolio manager to be successful. The average person does not have that level of education, history of past involvement, or amount of time to devote to their finances. Either stick with a passive fund, not a bad choice, or let a professional handle your portfolio management.

This choice also goes back to your risk tolerance. Again, passive funds are less risky and probably more appropriate for the general public. However, if you are comfortable or if you desire greater risk in hopes of more substantial gains, an active fund such as a target allocation fund may be appropriate. As you become more experienced with investing, you'll grow to find what is best for you. Your level of risk tolerance might not be immediately apparent, and it may change over the years your investment portfolio is growing. Choose your fund with care, but do so knowing you have options if you want to make a change later in life.

Chapter 10:

Too Little Investment

If there is one takeaway that retirement planners all can agree on, it is that the largest problem people typically face is not saving enough. Often, especially at the beginning of a person's career, they do not put away the requisite amount for their retirement, and, therefore, have to set aside significantly more money later in life.

While unfortunate, this pattern is not exactly surprising. When you are younger, retirement seems like a much less crucial concern. Something that is thirty years off is easy to underprepare for, and many people get tripped up by this short-term bias. It is, indeed, an observable psychological phenomenon dubbed "future time perspective." In an article titled, "Influence of future time perspective, financial knowledge, and financial risk tolerance on retirement saving behaviors" for Financial Services Review, Jay Jacobs-Lawson and Douglas Hershey describe this phenomenon. "Future time perspective is a psychological variable that receives a good deal of attention in the financial planning literature. It is a measure of the extent to which individuals focus on the future, rather than the present or past." Lawson and Hershey go on to explore a lengthy analysis on the relationship between successfully saving for retirement and an objective scale of a subject's ability to focus on the future—as well as their general financial knowledge and tolerance to risk in their savings portfolios. "Our findings indicate that future time perspective, financial knowledge, and financial risk tolerance are all important variables (both individually and in combination with one another) when it comes to understanding individuals' retirement saving practices."

In addition to the difficulty of focusing on the future over present-day concerns, a person who is twenty-six does not often hold a position for more than a few years. It is harder to budget and save when your income can fluctuate significantly year to year, if not more often. Financial volatility makes for a "shifting base" for a person's retirement to begin, and that changeability engenders weak foundations.

The unhappy side effect of poor early saving is the resulting missed opportunity. Your early years, while less financially productive, have the most earning potential due to the greater growth long-term investment provides. If you deposit $10 into an account and let it grow for three decades, it is going to be worth more than $10 you put in yesterday. The dollars you add in your twenties and thirties can have a much greater impact than what you save in your forties and fifties. Early saving is not something to neglect.

Of course, too little investment is not restricted to your early years. Many older adults underestimate how much they need to save for their retirement. In an article for the Journal of Economic Perspectives, "Are you sure you're saving enough for retirement?" Jonathan Skinner projected in 2007, "Many view the soon-to-retire Baby Boomers as woefully unprepared for their golden years. Bernheim (1992) suggested this cohort was saving just one-third of what they needed to retire comfortably. Christine Weller of the Economic Policy Institute stated that 'the average American household has virtually no chance to reach an adequate retirement savings in the next 50 years' (Dugas, 2002). One recent report declared 43 percent of American households 'at risk' of substantial declines in retirement income, even after factoring in financial and housing wealth (Munnell, Webb, and Delorme, 2006)."

The next wave of retirees, those in their forties and fifties right now, may face the same shortfall and resulting decline in quality of life that Skinner referred to ten years ago. A careful plan followed by disciplined saving can avoid the conclusion he reached. However, too little investment is a problem that many will face if this issue isn't taken as a serious problem. As previously stated, evaluate your finances, predict your needs later in life, and consistently reassess your position over time. Ask yourself the most important question, "When do I really want to retire?" That answer may change over time, as many people find they prefer to work longer. Don't immediately assume that you want the earliest possible retirement age; look inward before deciding that.

Chapter 11:

Market Volatility and Behavioral Finance

A common problem people encounter when dealing with finance is an inability to look at the big picture. Markets will have good days and bad ones; sometimes excellent days and terrible. That is predictable and even healthy. Unfortunately, people, even traders who are well-versed in macroeconomic behavior, often fall victim to a very human problem: when prices are going up, we assume they will always go up, and when prices are going down, we assume they are always going to go down. It takes conscious effort to fight this tendency.

That is not especially surprising, considering some studies in the field of behavioral finance indicate that this mindset is practically etched in our DNA. In "What is Behavioral Finance?" Victor Ricciardi and Helen Simon explain the science, "Behavioral finance attempts to explain and increase understanding of the reasoning patterns of investors, including the emotional processes involved and the degree to which they influence the decision-making process." It is a psychological and sociological approach to analyzing financial behavior in order to optimize the approach to money management, especially in an area as volatile as the stock market.

While the field covers numerous common behavior patterns, one that applies most closely to responses to market volatility is "financial cognitive dissonance." Ricciardi and Simon describe the theory of financial cognitive dissonance: "(The) theory of cognitive dissonance . . . states that people feel internal tension and anxiety when subjected to conflicting beliefs. As individuals, we attempt to reduce our inner conflict (decrease our dissonance) in one of two ways: 1) we change our past values, feelings, or opinions, or, 2) we attempt to justify or rationalize our choice. This theory may apply to investors or traders in the stock market who attempt to rationalize contradictory behaviors, so that they seem to follow naturally from personal values or viewpoints." Essentially, we give in to internal impulses that conflict with what we know to be true, and then justify it by altering original beliefs after the decision.

For instance, it is pure fact that markets can vary widely for days, weeks, and even months or years—and for better or worse. In the abstract, it is easy to understand and accept that idea. However, when you have money invested in a stock that is tanking for a few weeks, you might pull all your money out in violation of that idea. Afterward, you might slightly adjust that previously held belief to include a weak caveat that "it doesn't apply" in the given scenario. You change your belief to accommodate a decision instead of making a decision in response to a belief. When you fall victim to this problem, you erase all the knowledge you may have gained while educating yourself on how to invest. Learning about finance is only useful if you apply the principles you have studied. Success here is as much about willpower as it is about preparation.

Jay Ritter builds on these ideas in his article "Behavioral Finance" for the Pacific-Basin Finance Journal when he studies the litany of cognitive biases that influence buying and selling trends. "People underweight long-term averages. People tend to put too much weight on recent experience. This is sometimes known as the 'law of small numbers.' As an example, when equity returns have been high for many years (such as 1982–2000 in the US and western Europe), many people begin to believe that high equity returns are 'normal.'"

However, this problem is made more difficult by an opposite but equally damage fallacy, which Ritter calls "conservatism bias." Essentially, people begin to anchor their beliefs to a specific assumption, such as the quality of investments in a specific technological field, and they will not change those beliefs for anything. When that field experiences a setback and the "anchor breaks," they often overcorrect and cause themselves even more harm by totally eschewing the "anchor" and transferring all their cash into another area.

The fact is, rebalancing a portfolio to fit a changing market, which we will cover in the next chapter, is wise as long as you are careful and measured and you listen to expert advice. Reactionary buying and selling of huge percentages of your investments is never a good idea, especially if those transactions place a great deal of focus on a small portion of the market. However, a measured response to market trends will yield higher returns. Remember that there will always be trends, sometimes significant ones, and if you make any changes, don't do so too rapidly.

Chapter 12:

Disciplined Account Rebalance

Rebalancing your account is a crucial process to maintain a healthy makeup of funds, but it is often misunderstood. Basically, a rebalance is the process of periodically buying and selling some of the stocks that comprise your portfolio in accordance with the fluctuations in their price. It is a simple enough concept; what makes it difficult is its counterintuitive nature. Often, in a rebalance, you want to sell some of the assets that have done well recently and buy more of what is doing poorly. While this goes against many people's typical vision of "playing the stock market," it is crucial to maintaining your fund's level of risk.

We rebalance to maintain a diversified portfolio. Due to market volatility, fund composition is not stagnant. When you figure out your desired balance of stocks, bonds, and index funds, you have to work to maintain that ratio. For instance, to keep things simple, let's say you have a portfolio with two stocks (your real-life fund should have far more), and you want to keep the ratio of investment of each at 50%. After six months, stock A has done very well but stock B has lost value. To return to a 50% margin, you would need to sell some of stock A and buy more from stock B. While this may seem strange, there are two good reasons for doing so.

First, as stock A grows and stock B shrinks, your fund becomes less diversified. Risk is no longer divided evenly between the two. If stock A has 80% of the value of your portfolio, you will take a much bigger hit if stock A tanks. Rebalancing so that each stock covers an appropriate amount of your portfolio lowers risk, something that you need to manage carefully, especially in a retirement account.

Second, rebalancing allows you to buy low and sell high. You take advantage of an age-old stock market principle when you rebalance. If you sell portions of your portfolio that have done exceptionally well, you will make a nice profit. When you buy stocks that have not had recent success, you can get a lot of value for your money. If there is one surety about the stock market, it is that it's unpredictable. While selling a stock that has performed well may seem counterintuitive, it could easily lose value after you sell it. The opposite is true for a stock that has had a few bad months. Warren Buffet notably has said, "Be greedy when everyone is fearful, and fearful when everyone is greedy." Follow this advice and you will make a tidy profit.

Types of Rebalancing

There are different ways to consider rebalancing your portfolio, and experts are still engaged in a debate about which is optimal. For instance, when rebalancing, should you do an exact rebalance, or rebalance within a range? When stock A grows to 80% of your portfolio, do you bring it down all the way to 50%, or accept having it between 50% and 55% while it is growing so well?

Maybe more importantly is deciding how much flexibility you give your equity before rebalancing it. Most people set times of the year to rebalance. If you are set to rebalance your stocks in June, but stock A has exploded in April, should you wait those extra months to make a change? In the past, a sudden rise in price has sometimes anticipated an equally rapid fall. An extra layer of complication, which some strategies address, is whether you respond differently to assets growing than you do to them shrinking. Some studies show that giving extra leeway to issues that are improving is a wise choice.

You will find many people differing on these opinions. When you start rebalancing your profile, it is time to consult an expert who can give you a long-term strategy. However, absent the luxury of personal expert help, the key principle at play here is consistency. Do not allow for too much flexibility in a portfolio. If you have set your balance at 60/40 stocks to bonds, some might consider letting it stay around 70/30 because an issue is doing well to be a good strategy, but it is really just ignoring your original intentions and setting aside the wisdom of an account rebalance. When in doubt, take the conservative option. It will save you from reckless behavior, and when saving for retirement, avoiding unnecessary risk is favorable. If you are disciplined enough and consistent enough with your rebalancing behavior, you will induce strong long-term growth. Set an initial balance of stocks and bonds and maintain it, updating every quarter or so.

Rebalancing vs. Other Strategies

Rebalancing is one of three widely acknowledged strategies in fund management. The second is free-floating, the opposite of rebalancing, in which little management occurs and equal contributions are consistently made across the board; stocks that perform well are allowed to take on an increasingly great portion of a portfolio The third is market timing, in which asset allocation is set by attempting to predict short-term market trends.

There are notable problems with these last two strategies, especially when it comes to managing a retirement account, where security and steady long-term growth are important. A free-floating strategy essentially forgoes any semblance of an effort to diversify a portfolio. Stocks that do well for a year or two can eventually eclipse most other equities you are managing. The risk here often is extremely high. Unpredictable markets can wipe out large portions of a fund if a single stock with a good track record takes a major hit. One scandal or drought or innovative competitor can destroy the value of a stock, and if that stock has free-floated its way to a large percentage of your retirement account, you have a big problem. It cannot be said enough: in a retirement account, diversification is your friend. Free-floating also denies your ability to strategize your portfolio. The laissez-faire, hands-off approach means no buying low or selling high.

An investment strategy based around market timing is much more complex, but often a poor decision. Trading by anticipating short-term trends is a job for professionals, and even they make mistakes. It requires serious attention and a bit of luck to make money this way, something that most people do not have. While it can be fun to play the stock market, this sort of gamble is difficult to pull off yourself. Rebalancing your retirement account is safer and far easier.

The Research

Research shows that market timing, while it can yield the greatest dividends in some cases, underperforms rebalancing overall. And, while free-floating shows occasional advantages in average gain, risk is significantly higher, making it untenable for a retirement account policy.

In the Financial Services Review, John Knight and Lewis Mandel published "Nobody Gains from Dollar Cost Averaging, Numerical and Empirical Results." Their results indicated that optimal rebalancing performed better overall than dollar-cost averaging—another type of market timing—and buy-and-hold—another term for a free-floating strategy. "Relative to the investor who uses Optimal Rebalancing both the investor using Dollar Cost Averaging and the investor who Buys and Holds may be seen to experience utility loss, regardless of the degree of risk aversion." Simply put, no matter what level of risk you are comfortable with, rebalancing will yield better results.

In "Do Firms Rebalance their Capital Structures," Mark Leary and Michael Roberts write, "The evidence in support of dynamic rebalancing is quite strong; almost all of the empirical predictions are verified by the estimation results . . . [rebalancing effects] are both highly statistically and economically significant."

Finally, a 2007 study on long-term pension growth "Stock market performance and pension fund investment policy: rebalance, free float, or market timing" by Jacob Bikker, Dirk Broeders, and Jan de Dreu corroborated this, stating, "The value added of market timing is limited and consequently pension funds would do better by spending resources on deriving the best strategic asset allocation strategy and to use rebalancing to invest accordingly."

(Note: In the interest of clarity, research does indicate that, while small to average-sized funds studied here behave similarly to retirement accounts, consistent scheduled rebalancing is less effective for very large funds.)

There is a great deal of investigation into the subject of rebalancing and other strategies, and that no doubt will continue. However, overall, the research suggests it is the best strategy for a retirement account. Debate on the specifics of rebalancing techniques is ongoing as well. If you can rebalance several times a year, that is probably ideal. Small transaction costs exist for rebalancing, and you should avoid too many if possible. Regardless of exact frequency, regular rebalancing is a crucial part of managing a retirement portfolio.

Chapter 13:

Putting Short-Term Needs Second to Long-Term Savings

As we have said, managing your money within a budget is key to planning for retirement and reaching your 401(k) targets. Creating a plan, sticking to it, and reviewing it consistently is necessary. The "sticking to it" aspect is where discipline comes in. Setting aside some of your immediate desires to allow for future prosperity is the cornerstone of good saving behavior. Dieting is a similar process. Likely, at some point during the new year, you or someone you know may decide to go on a diet. The success or failure of that diet will hinge on the ability to resist a slice of cake or big breakfast—in other words, to put off direct wants in favor of a long-term target.

In "The Role of Self-Regulation, Future Orientation, and Financial Knowledge in Long-Term Financial Decisions," Elizabeth Howlett, Jeremy Kees, and Elyria Kemp write, "Consumers must restrain themselves and resist temptation to spend money in the short term in order to maximize their financial well-being in the long term." They continue to realize the conclusion that financial literacy, especially when aided by a professional consultant, is the key to correct saving behavior. A real understanding of different types of plans, your future needs, and especially the power of long-term compounding growth will lead people to begin saving earlier in life and make them less likely to withdraw unnecessarily.

Seeing the Whole Picture

The key to maintaining a productive mindset conducive to saving enough money is to always focus on the "bigger picture." A few dollars here or there might not seem like much, but remember that $50 now is going to be $100 or $120 when you retire. That money might go toward paying travel expenses while you vacation in your favorite countries, financing your grandkid's college tuition, or helping pay for a child's wedding. The longer you save your money, the more influence it can have over your life or the life of someone you care about.

Seeing the bigger picture is easier when you have actual goals for what you are going to do with your savings. During the budget-making process, think of tangible uses for the money, not just obscure luxury items. It is significantly easier to save when you can think, "This is going to pay for a sailboat when I retire" instead of "This is money so I will have financial freedom." Vague concepts will never motivate you like specific ideas can.

Chapter 14:

Leaving an Employer

Since the innovation of the modern retirement account in the 1950s, the average duration of a person's time working with an employer has significantly decreased. The Bureau of Labor Statistics has the current worker staying with a full-time job for an average of slightly over four years, significantly lower than long-term positions used to be. This change in the way people work is not necessarily bad or good, but it adds an extra layer when trying to understand the subtleties of 401(k) management, specifically, what to do if you accumulate more than one 401(k). Generally, it is a wise option to roll the balance of an old 401(k) into an active IRA and take that opportunity to diversify your portfolio.

There are numerous reasons for this. First, company-managed 401(k)s often feature tame, low-yield investment profiles. You will not see the full potential of your money by leaving it sitting around in an account with an old employer. A well-funded retirement is about efficiently using the money you have saved. Inviting enough risk to incite a reasonable reward is necessary if you want to meet your monetary needs when you end your work life.

Another factor to consider is that managing many small 401(k)s is more work than handling a few larger accounts. If you accumulate three 401(k)s and you have a partner that does the same, that's six accounts to keep track of for the family finances, six accounts that are made up of numerous smaller investments. That is a lot of information to stay on top of. Saving for retirement is difficult enough without having to repeat your task several times.

Numerous accounts also mean a higher number of transaction fees. Manipulating and maintaining a 401(k) carries various fees with it, and while they are light relative to the program's benefits, there is no need to take on more than necessary.

Preparing to Leave

Setting up your 401(k) to roll over to another retirement account is only part of the process of leaving an employer. It is a major move, and it will have a significant effect on your finances, saving for retirement especially. Long-term saving understandably often takes a backseat to short-term needs; however, if you plan sensibly, leaving an employer doesn't have to mean suspending your saving.

Ideally, when you leave an employer, you have another job waiting for you (this chapter is not directed at people who are retiring). Before committing to a transition, look over your financial plan. If your goal is to save a certain amount of money before you retire, how does your new job compare? That does not only apply to salary but to their retirement benefits. Does the new job match contributions to a 401(k)? How much flexibility do you have in the investment portfolio? Is there a physical toll associated with the new job that may raise medical costs later in life?

If you don't have a job lined up and are leaving your workplace for other reasons, you should consider the effect that months of noninvestment can have on the returns you need to have when you retire. It can be profound, and you should consider higher savings once you are employed again to make up for lost time.

When you are preparing to leave a job, you should probably speak to an expert who can break down everything you need to consider. There are too many variables to address in situations such as these, and you should not gamble with your retirement planning. It is too vital and too nuanced. Failing that, if you are not in a financial spot to pay for consultation or you simply do not have the time, at least make sure to be careful when making your decision.

Cashing Out a 401(k)

If you choose not to roll over or maintain your 401(k) and instead withdraw all the money early, also known as cashing out, you should know what you are getting into. Aside from the obvious losses to your investment portfolio and therefore future retirement account, as previously stated, you will certainly get hit with significant fees that you should be aware of before making this decision. With early withdrawal penalties, federal taxes, and state taxes, you will likely be left with between half and two-thirds of what was in the account prior to cashing out.

In some situations, for instance when you leave a job you have only had for a short time and the 401(k) is not substantial, it might seem more inviting and natural to simply cash out the account. However, regardless, you will be losing a substantial portion of the money you have saved. Even an investment of only $5,000 would get cut down to $3,000 or even lower, and that is money that could be far more valuable to you when it has grown for decades and you are ready to retire.

The decision to cash out a 401(k) early is never something you should do on a whim. Unless you need income immediately, there is no good reason not to roll it over into a new account or simply leave it alone and let it grow while you continue to work and contribute to other accounts. Having multiple 401(k)s can even help diversify your retirement portfolio by spreading investments out over a larger group of issues.

Part 3:
Using a 401(k) and Post Retirement

Chapter 15:

Planning after Retirement

After decades of hard work saving portions of each paycheck, you will, eventually retire. Whether the end of your work life comes in your late fifties, sixties, or even seventies, you need to have a plan ready for how to spend the money you have accumulated. Planning is crucial in the earning stage of 401(k) management but equally important, if not more so, during the spending phase. Once you retire, it is difficult to return to a working life. The capital you have in your retirement account, or accounts, is pretty much all you will be able to live your life on. So you can't go into the process unprepared.

However, while this life stage should clearly be a priority when planning out finances, many people who devote plenty of time deciding how much to save do not put nearly as much thought into how they are going to spend. A recent survey from the RAND Center for the Study of Aging, "Building Up, Spending Down: Financial Literacy, Retirement Savings Management, and Decumulation" found that, of a sample of people who considered themselves well-prepared for retirement, only 28% thought about how they were going to spend their money year to year following retirement, and less than half of those people developed and refined a specific plan. While saving for retirement does require a lot of planning, focus, and knowledge, spending is not a simple process, and it often goes overlooked.

The same report cited a clear link between financial literacy and lack of postretirement planning. Many people who work hard and learn about saving for retirement are financially literate by the time they retire. However, these people often are the same retirees who do not know how to spend their money. "We find that our financial literacy measures predict planning for spending down money in retirement, even though our respondents report that they are not well prepared for decumulation in the retirement phase. However, despite the relationship between financial literacy and retirement planning, we find that our financial literacy measures do not strongly predict retirement preparedness, as measured by size of DC plan accounts or total retirement savings." This connection speaks to some level of overconfidence on the part of people who have saved well. Everyone must enter retirement with the knowledge that, while their work life may have ended, they still have many long-term financial considerations to think through.

There are numerous factors to consider when spending what you have saved. While these are probably things you thought about during the saving process, as usual, reassessment is your friend. You will have a much clearer picture of your health costs, your general living expenses, and what luxuries you are looking for once on "the other side" of retirement saving, so to speak.

Unfortunately, there is an added variable during retirement spending that is difficult to reconcile. You never know how long you are going to live or how much your late-stage medical costs might be. Most people do not want to leave half of their savings unspent, and no one wants to run out of money before the end of their life and have nothing to support themselves. It is a difficult puzzle to figure out, especially because few people enjoy considering their own death, especially not estimating when it will be. But the task set before every retiree is to estimate how long they will live, and to plan accordingly.

Many seem to have something of a poor revelation upon their financial assessment at retirement. In "The Retirement Consumption Puzzle: Anticipated and Actual Declines in Spending at Retirement," Michael Hurd and Susann Rohwedder find that, "Overall, our results pose a significant challenge to the validity of standard life cycle models. Instead, they appear to suggest that on average individuals who arrive at retirement with few resources experience a 'surprise'—they take stock of their finances only to discover that their resources are insufficient to maintain their accustomed standards of living (e.g. because pension income is less than expected, or because they recognize that savings will go less far than they had hoped), and they revise their expectations downward in light of this realization." Many people do not accurately assess their postretirement needs and rapidly spend more than they should.

This is another situation in which professional financial advice is probably the right idea. You need a clear picture of your fiscal resources and how to allocate them—someone to coach you through the difficult aspects of your career. This section is about augmenting that hands-on advice with personal education to make you more a more financially literate and effective saver.

Chapter 16:

Withdrawing from Your 401(k)

Of course, one of the first steps to your postretirement life is accessing the money you have saved and beginning withdrawals. There are numerous caveats and details specific to each retiree. If, for instance, you retire before the age of fifty-nine and a half, withdrawing money from a 401(k) comes with fees attached. As we have discussed before, these extra fees are one of the many reasons premature withdrawals are a bad option that should be left for emergencies only. For those who want to retire early, savings should be in a more traditional investment portfolio that does not have caveats attached to early withdrawals.

When you do actually withdraw money from your 401(k), you need to be careful how much you take out. Taking out more than you need will negatively impact your finances, as the money left in your retirement account is still invested and so will continue to grow. A hefty withdrawal early on will not only deplete your account, but it will cut away at long-term interest.

Not surprisingly, views on how much to withdraw per year vary among the finance community. Commonly, experts advise 4%

withdrawal every year to meet your needs while maintaining your account's integrity. However, others suggest that 7% is still within the range of reasonable withdrawals. Still others advise keeping withdrawals as low as 3% to maintain long-term financial security. It is a balancing act. Withdrawing a higher percentage of your savings will make you more comfortable in the short term and perhaps help you achieve some of your retirement goals, but it leaves you vulnerable to problems later in life. Again, your age heavily restricts your ability to earn money, and that restriction only increases as you grow older; this, while your likelihood of serious medical problems goes up.

Deciding on what percentage to withdraw from your account per year depends on numerous factors that you need to plan for. If, for instance, you want to travel soon after retirement while you are still physically able, maybe you start by taking out 6–7% and taper back in your later years. On the other hand, maybe you have genetic dispositions to medical problems that only manifest late in life. In that case, you might want to stick to simple domestic leisure and only withdraw 3–4% to begin with. Further considerations might include whether you are single or married, whether you plan on living in a retirement community or a normal residence, or what hobbies you want to pursue.

In their 2003 paper, "How to spend and invest retirement savings," Aparna Gupta and Walter Murray write, "The problem of saving for retirement and that of consuming retirement savings after retirement have very different characteristics, and there is merit in modeling them differently. Moreover, a retiree is more motivated to take an interest in how best to invest since the consequences are immediate."

They consider that creating clear solutions for postretirement spending problems is more difficult than preretirement savings, largely because the "planning horizon," or end date, is unknown. "We advocate solving the problem with non-uniform time periods. This formulation allows for a finer time-refinement for periods at the beginning of the planning period. This feature is particularly attractive when the problem is solved on a rolling basis, since it gives a better resolution on decisions that are immediately implemented, while limiting the growth in the number of variables." More simply, it is correct to reevaluate your spending patterns with an expert on a regular basis, given that the variables that affect how much of your retirement savings you should spend will change regularly and maybe unpredictably. While rules of thumb are helpful to set basic saving patterns, they are risky when applied long term without a great deal of thought. Spending might seem like the easy part of retirement, but in reality, it is one of the most precarious. Understanding and remembering this can be key to financial security late in life.

Where to Withdraw From

For many years, a trite piece of advice was prevalent in the investing world. It was this: "To find the percentage of stocks that should make up your account balance, simply subtract your age from one hundred." Of course, no aspect of finance is that simple or broadly applicable. The advice stuck around because it was catchy and it did accomplish the goal of reinforcing an important principle: the older you get, the more your portfolio should be made up of bonds. Secure issues that will yield a little return and more importantly keep your savings steady should be your goal. When you start hitting age eighty and ninety, your portfolio balance should not still be at a 60/40 stock/bond split.

Your withdrawals should reflect this principle. To state the obvious, selling off funds will alter the percentage of stocks and bonds within a portfolio. With that in mind, when you begin to sell portions of your portfolio, keep a careful eye on what the makeup of your holdings will be after your sale. Selling a large number of bonds introduces a great deal of risk into a portfolio. If you are not careful, you may end up in a precarious financial situation and not realize it.

Chapter 17:

Social Security

The final piece of the postretirement financial puzzle is Social Security, the steadiest segment of your income and, for better or worse, the one least under your control. For those who do not know, Social Security is a program whereby the federal government provides some financial security to retirees by giving them a stipend for necessary life expenses, such as medical and housing costs. Social Security is not meant to ensure a life of luxury, but it does keep people who are unable to work out of dire financial straits.

Knowing your Social Security benefit in advance is key to a sound plan. See the site www.ssa.gov to begin looking at your future benefits. Many people who retire before age sixty-six need higher income from their 401(k), and, once Social Security kicks in, the 401(k) distributions can scale back.

Social Security should not make up a majority of your money later in life. If you have saved well, Social Security will supplement your income but not override it as your main means of support. When it comes to Social Security, mostly you will just be cashing the checks. However, government policy regarding Social Security, especially in a population that is growing older due to medical advances and with a new generation who is having fewer kids, may end up changing. There is not a lot to say right now about where Social Security might go. It could rise, fall, stay the same, or be converted into a different program.

Unfortunately, if you want a book that can predict the future, you've come to the wrong place. The best advice is to stay alert and informed about the condition of your Social Security. It may change substantially, and you do not want to be caught unaware. If you're lucky, nothing unexpected will occur, and Social Security will still be a simple, regular buffer for your retirement savings. However, be on the lookout for that to change, because it is certainly a possibility.

Conclusion

Whether you are lazily crushing sand between your toes on a breezy afternoon at the beach, unaware of the time; swatting your first drive of the fifteenth hole of the day at a golf course, probably also unaware of the time; traveling the world sitting in first class on your frequent flyer miles; walking your dog in the park; playing with grandchildren; taking new courses at the local college; or whatever your ideal vision of retirement is, you probably got there with a sturdy retirement account. You won't have the freedom to do what you what in your golden years if you don't spend time and money right now preparing for those years. That means saving consistently and spending conservatively sometimes. That means learning about bonds and stocks, talking to experts, and putting in time to educating yourself. That means checking emotions at the door. That means setting a plan and sticking to it.

As this book has said before, the whole process is about discipline. That discipline comes in many forms. It's the discipline required to first sit down and make a realistic schedule. It's the discipline to regularly save enough money and to be realistic about how you are doing at approaching your goals. It's the discipline to maintain your profile in the face of an economic downturn or to change it even if things are going well. It's the discipline of sticking to a rebalancing schedule and of staying educated. The final level of discipline comes when you must keep your spending steady after you retire.

That discipline has to come from somewhere. There needs to be a source, an idea you can draw on to keep yourself engaged in best practices—your reason to save. For some people, the idea might be a worst-case scenario. Maybe, if they don't save enough for retirement, they will have to live their final years uncomfortable or even unable to pay for necessary medical costs, ending up a drain on their families without the freedom to live how they want to.

However, focusing on the negative is likely a bad choice. Your reason to save is something you'll think about a lot over the years, and while fear is a good motivator, it's also corrosive. If you dwell on something fearful to the exclusion of all else for too long, you will never be able to relax, no matter how well you save. Instead, focus on the positive. Focus on the possibilities retirement can bring. For so much of your life, time was a major limiting factor. There was that certain thing that you never had enough vacation days for. Now that time is available, and given a little money, you have a chance to something special.

Again, what that "very special" thing is will change drastically based on the person who is doing the dreaming. However, it is essential to find your version. Without a dream to motivate you, all the work that you need to maintain for years will never get done. If you say to yourself, "I'm doing this so I have enough money after I retire," it's unlikely you'll get to where you need to be. However, if you tell yourself, "I'm doing this so I can travel through Europe" or "I'm doing this so I can see every basketball stadium," your chances of staying disciplined on retirement behavior become much higher.

So, if you haven't already, take a day, a week, or a month—however long you need—and find your retirement goal. Think of the goal that you can focus on over the years to keep yourself on the straight and narrow. Think of what you can focus on so you keep putting that money away into your 401(k) every paycheck. Perform a disciplined account rebalance every quarter, diligently manage your investment portfolio, stay up to date with your original retirement plan, and do everything you need to do to put the OK in 401(k).

Made in the USA
Monee, IL
04 November 2026

67385510R00049